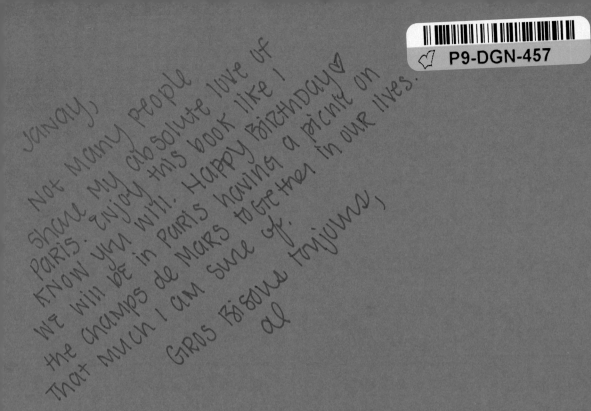

Janay,

Not many people
share my absolute love of
Paris. Enjoy this book like I
know you will. Happy Birthday♡
We will be in Paris having a picnic on
the Champs de Mars together in our lives.
That much I am sure of.

Gros Bisous Toujours,
al

PARIS IN LOVE

PARIS IN LOVE

Nichole Robertson

CHRONICLE BOOKS

SAN FRANCISCO

Library of Congress Cataloging-in-Publication Data available.

ISBN 978-1-4521-3318-8

Manufactured in China

Design by Kristen Hewitt

10 9 8 7 6 5 4 3

Chronicle Books LLC
680 Second Street
San Francisco, California 94107
www.chroniclebooks.com

DEDICATION

To anyone who has fallen in love with a place

INTRODUCTION

Falling in love with a place is similar to falling in love with a person. Although it's the superficial things that grab your attention first, over time you notice the subtle details that make the object of your affection irresistible. Little by little, those tiny details add up to something more, something difficult to define, something all-consuming. You go from curiosity to fondness to infatuation and then it hits you: You're in love.

My first book, *Paris in Color*, documents my own process of falling in love with Paris. Over several years, I recorded the details I loved and that defined the city for me. I used color as a means of filtering out distractions and evoking distinct moods. When Paris wore yellow, she cheered me up. The verdant greens of the trees along the promenades calmed me down. Black evoked a sense of mystery, sophistication, and secrecy.

On the days I hadn't decided what I'd photograph, I'd leave it up to chance. After a few minutes, a certain color would grab my attention. It always surprised me that this color, which moments before had gone unnoticed, was suddenly everywhere. And there was one color that had a unique way of dominating, of always grabbing my eye:

Red. Rich, sanguine red.

Red demands your attention. Red draws you in. Whether it's a towering metro sign, a bold door, or a tiny tangle of flowers in a window box that lures you from the end of a long street, when Paris wears red, she seduces.

I wondered if Paris's come-hither reds could tell a visual story of falling in love with the city. I wanted to capture the natural rhythm of red as I walked Paris's streets from morning to night. I submitted to the color, and let it guide me from arrondissement to arrondissement. From worn facades to mopeds, wine glasses to café signs, each detail drew me a little closer. When night fell, the mood changed, and my attention shifted to red light, often intimate, always inviting.

What strikes me most as I reflect on the project is that the collection is greater than the sum of its parts. Like words in a sentence, no individual photo stands on its own. They work together as a love story of sorts, and although some subjects may feel more obvious than others—a graffiti heart, a bouquet of flowers—they are no more or less important than the objects beside them—cane chairs and stop lights. In fact, it was often the unexpected I liked the most. But isn't that just like love—discovery and surprise?

The photos in this book are arranged to mimic that slow walk from morning to night. The city is dressed up in her most lustrous reds like a new dress for a first date.

What happens next is between you and Paris.

Au Petit Bougnat

Petit déjeuner

Café·Thé·Chocolat

Vin au verre

Plat du Jour

Apéritifs·Bières·Sodas

Onion soup

LES BOISSONS
DU BOUGNAT
Les aperitifs

LE MATIN

SUCRE

Kris

Gino
and
Jennifer
9.9.13

D + N

À l'écoute de tous vos moments
de convivialité
Cocktails . Réceptions . Plateaux Repas

Horaires d'Ouverture de 8 h à 19 h
fermé le lundi

60541 · A. DE BOYNES 0688603097

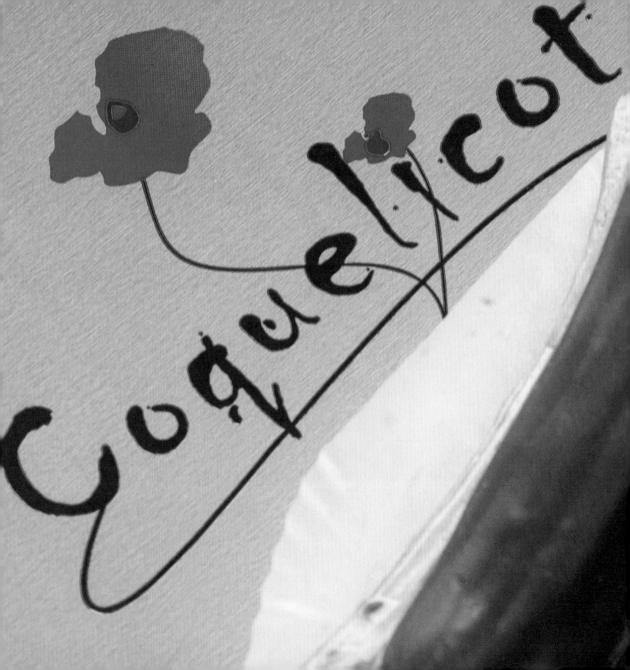

Glaces artisanales
· Maison Pedone ·

cornet simple   2,80 €
······· double   4,00 €
······· triple   5,50 €
Supplement Chantilly 0,50 €

Glaces: café Brésilien,
caramel au beurre salé,
pistache pure Suite,
chocolat grand cru Valrhona,
vanille gousse Bourbon

Brasserie Sorbe

L'APRÈS-MIDI

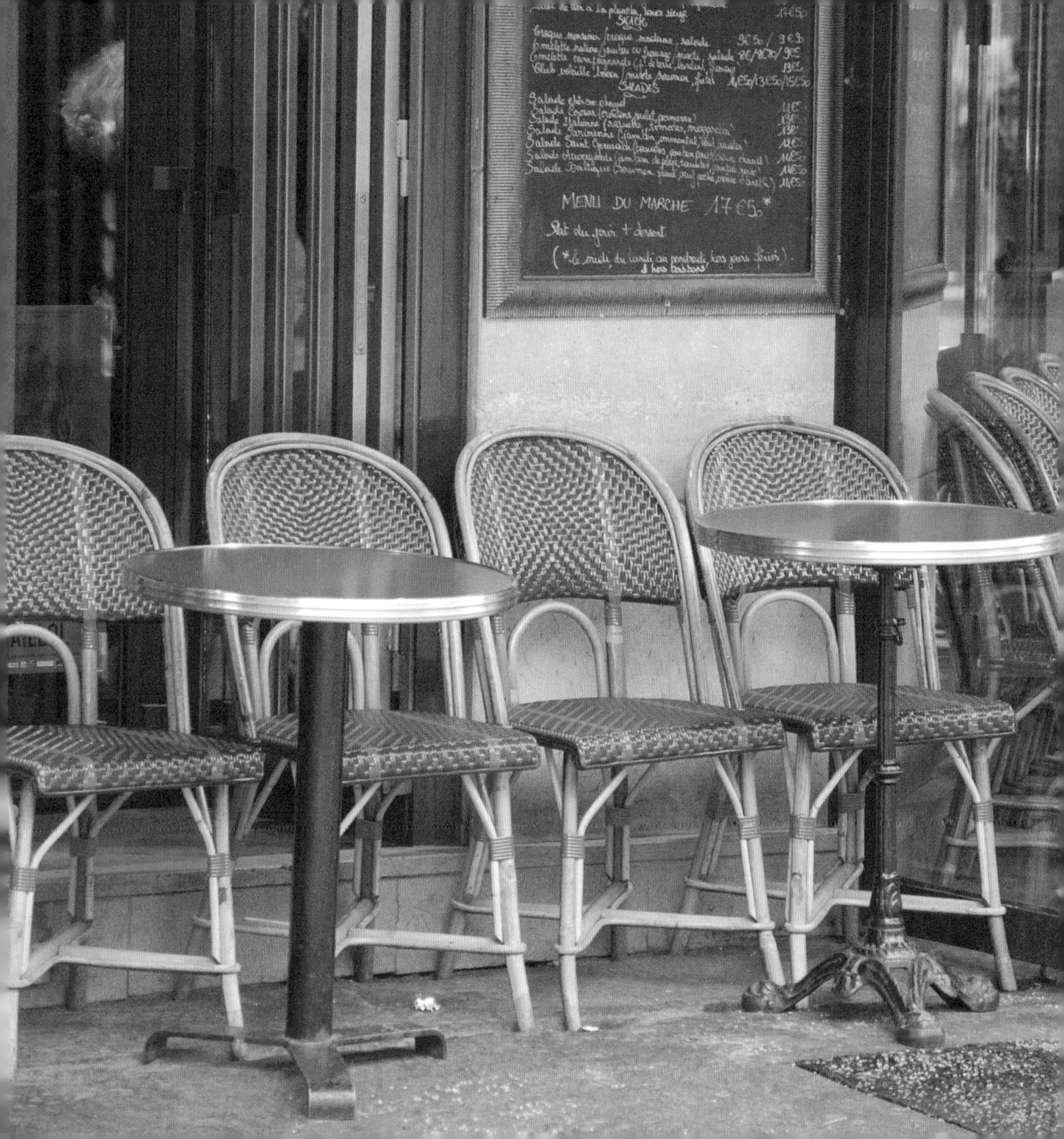
SNACK
SALADES
MENU DU MARCHE 17€50*
Plat du jour + dessert

Glaces artisanales

· Maison Pedone ·

cornet simple	2,80 €	
. . . . . double	4,00 €	
. . . . triple	5,50 €	
Supplement Chantilly	0,50 €	

Glaces : café Brésilien,
caramel au beurre salé,
pistache pure Sicile,
chocolat grand cru Valrhona,
vanille gousse Bourbon

j'irai fleurir mes rêves

Fred Le Chevalier

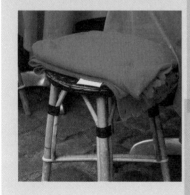

AU
CRÉPUSCULE

Le verre _____ 3€50

50 cl. _____ 9€00

75 cl. _____ 11€00

Boissons fraiches

Thé, Café glacés

Cocktails   8€00

Les bières

1664   pression 4€00

prix nets

Possibilité Soda,
Jus de fruits et
Bière 50 cl.

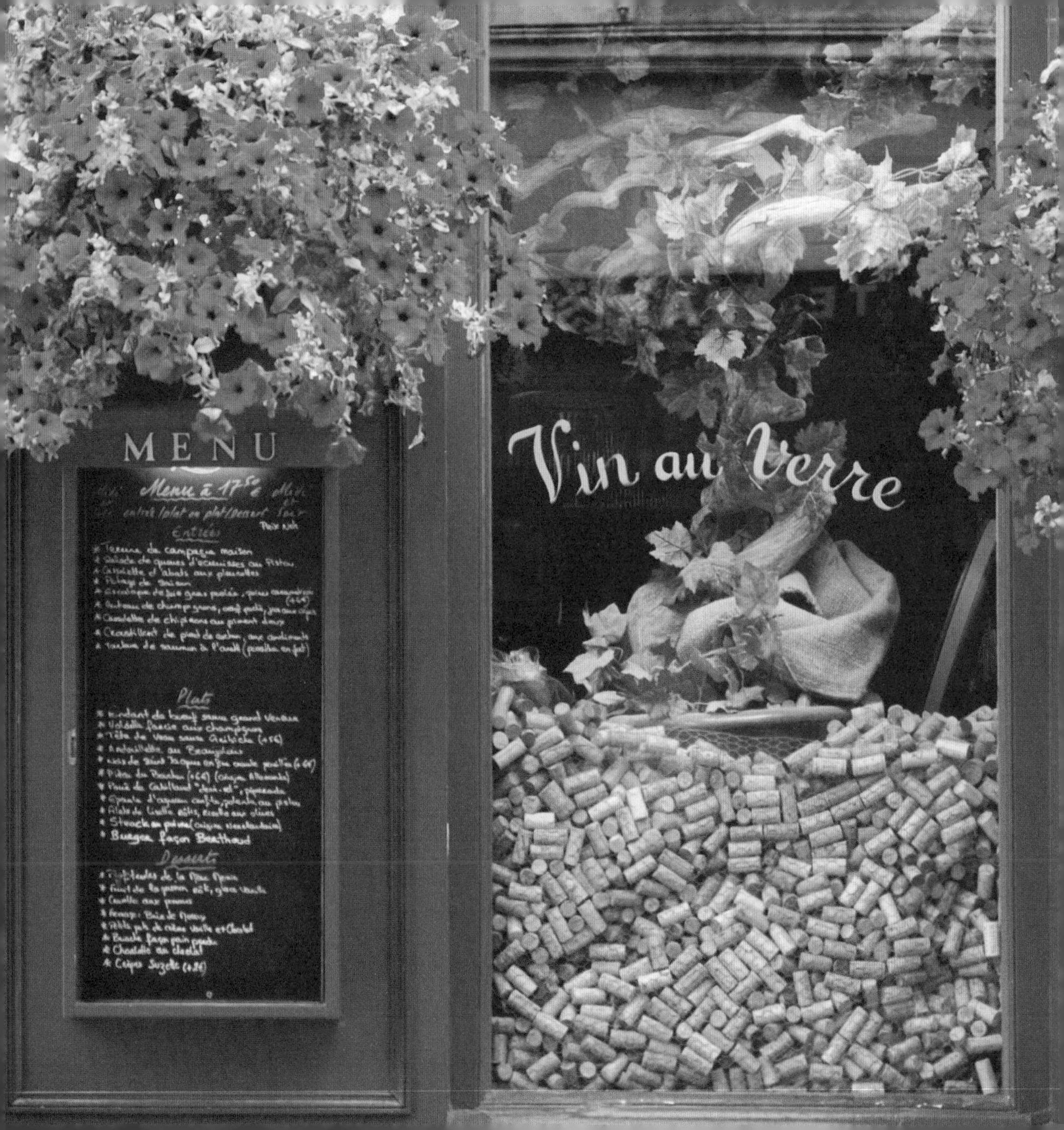
MENU
Vin au Verre

Drôle d'Endroit Pour Une Rencontre

RÔLE D'ENDROIT POUR UNE RE

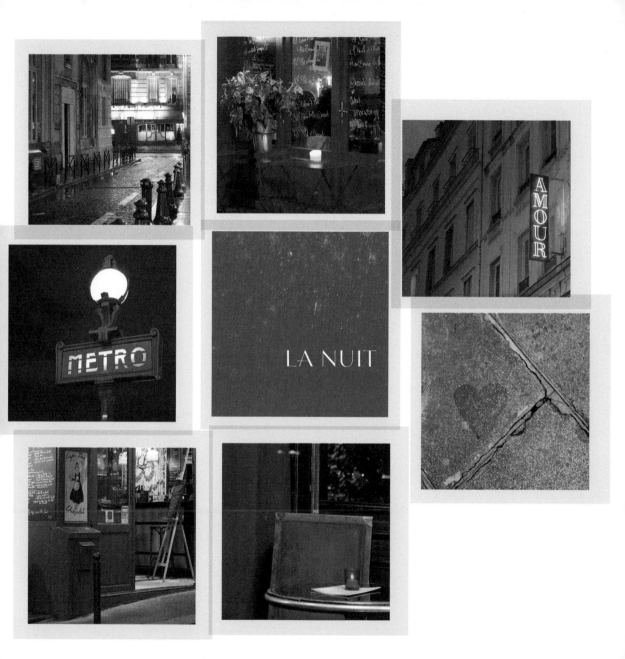

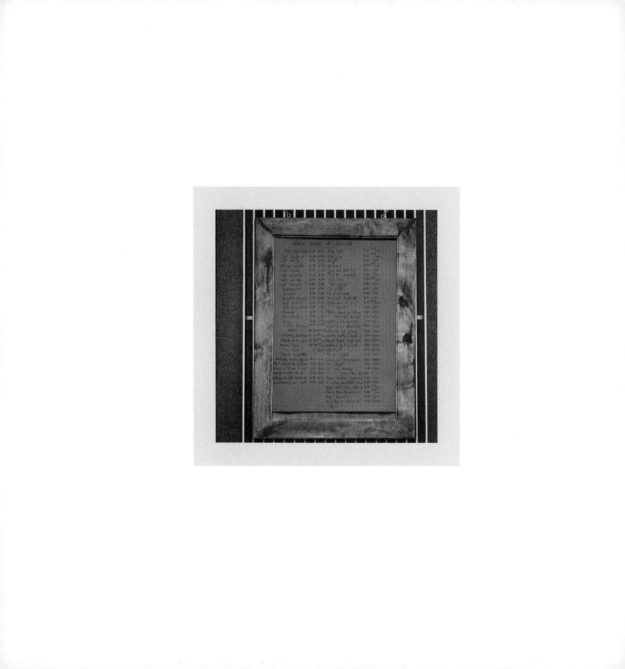

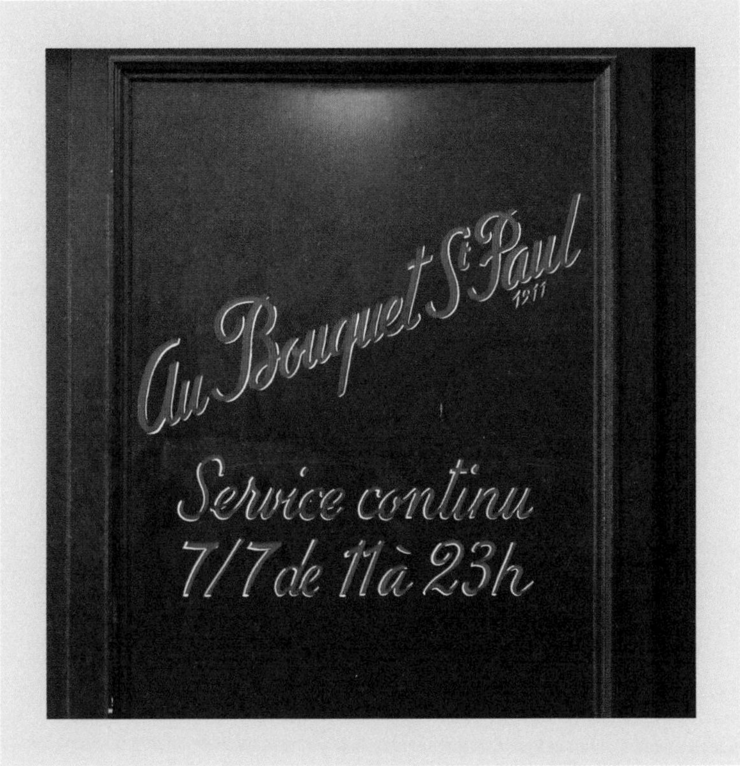
Au Bouquet St Paul
1911
Service continu
7/7 de 11 à 23h

...toes, cheese, bacon

...te de bœuf +3,50€

Rib of beef

...on de lait grillé

Sucking pig

...m frais sauce bearnaise

...h bearnaise sauce